HOPE OVER ANXIETY WORKBOOK!

How to Smash Crippling Fear and Live a Life You Will Love!

A self-help and workbook. A memoir. Your guide.

My journey to wellness. How I found hope and made my way to having a life I have only dreamed of and how I want to help you on your journey too!

CHRISTOPHER MOSS

Disclaimer

My book *Hope over Anxiety Workbook* is to coach and guide you on your journey. From crippling anxiety to living a life you will love. It is to help you develop yourself in to the person I know you can be.

This book deals with a lot of hard topics. It is meant to be inspiring. It is not intended to replace professional help. It is here to coach and guide you. To see anxiety in another way. To see your life differently.

This is designed to be informative and educational. It does not replace medical judgments or considered therapy or other higher treatments.

I am unable to respond to specific questions or comments about your personal situation, diagnosis or treatment. I am also unable to give any clinical opinions. If you are in urgent need of assistance I would advise you to contact your local emergency services, or local mental health crisis hotlines.

My resources mentioned in this book are used to help and guide you. It is for education and information only. I am not a medical professional. Please do not replace my information for the specialised training and professional judgement of a health care or mental health care professional.

Neither the author nor publisher can be held responsible for the use of the information detailed in this book.

I would highly recommend consulting a trained professional before making any calls regarding treatment of yourself or others.

My promise to you. If you follow this book you will:

Feel calmer. You will have control over your thoughts. You will understand yourself and your triggers. You will be self-confident and resilient. You will be happier and more positive. You will know what life you want and how to get it. You will feel inspired and believe you will be anxiety free!

A Challenge to You

You will learn all the skills and gain insight into who you are. You will be empowered and inspired.

I have laid this book out so you can become the best you. I would love to see you become anxiety free. It is possible if you follow my workbook. Are you up for the challenge?

If you succeed. Would you share your story with me? I would love to hear about it!

Email me at mosschristopher799@gmail.com

Table of Contents

About the Author

Christopher Moss is married with two children. He lives in Northamptonshire, England. He has worked in retail for over 30 years. He is a store manager.

His first three books *HOPE OVER ANXIETY, FREEDOM OVER ANXIETY* and *POWER OVER ANXIETY* are all best-sellers.

He has helped thousands of people through his books. He wants to help you too.

He has a passion for writing, building life skills and inspiring others to take control of their anxiety. His mission is to give people who are suffering the skills and tools so they can break free on their own. To create a life they want. To utilise the skills they have from anxiety, to be the best version of them they can be.

Hope:

'A feeling of expectation and desire
for a particular thing to happen.'
Synonyms: aspiration, desire, wish,
expectation, ambition, aim, plan, dream.
'A feeling of trust.'
—Dictionary. Com

'Hope is the only thing stronger than fear.'
—Suzanne Collins

Look in the mirror, feel excited, full of hope, determination and say:

I AM going to break free of anxiety. I AM going to be the person I always wanted. I AM stronger than I think I am!

What does the feeling of having broken anxiety feel like? My experience.

The first few months were a little weird. It's like losing a part of your body. Feeling it's there, having the twinges then checking and finding it's gone! It was surreal.

Sometimes I would see one of my triggers coming up and expect an anxiety attack or blind panic to escape over me. I would breathe in deeply but slowly, expecting the onslaught. Close my eyes, ready for the whirlwind to hit me. BANG! But there was no bang. I would open my eyes and there would be no feelings of worry. I wouldn't feel powerless. I felt okay. I would stop breathing deeply. I would feel a little silly for expecting the onslaught.

It was like the end few months of a war. A war that had lasted a lifetime. A painful and damaging experience. I had tamed my anxiety. I could see it for what it was. I had exposed the huge imposing monster, with its powers have waned considerably.

Sometimes anxiety raises its ugly head and can ambush me. But I know that I am leaning on the edge of my comfort zone and that I have upgraded my challenges, so it's okay. I can be kind to myself. I think *'how can I handle it better next time? Don't worry about it. Move on.'* I have spent a lifetime giving myself a hard time. I am human. Learn and improve.

I would feel less tired. I would feel happier. My mind wasn't so rapid. I became more creative. I was kinder to myself. I could catch a negative thought, an old ace my anxiety would use to get me off my watching point (I will discuss this later) and drag me down to its level. Trying to get me lost in the pain and the worry.

But I wouldn't get off my place. I would acknowledge the feeling and let it go. Like a balloon floating off into the distance. Note and let go.

I got to the point when I could manipulate my anxiety. To get me pushing on and doing things. To be driven and determined. To have that edge at work but at a cost to my family.

I went past that point as I stopped my caffeine intake and slept better. This sets new challenges.

My life is so much better. I have a way to go to be anxiety free. But the burden I carried is gone.

This is a brief look at what happened to me. And it all started with HOPE.

Do you want to feel this too?

Introduction - Are You Ready?

It's been a few years since I wrote the original *Hope over Anxiety* book. What an amazing journey! Four books on — three in seven weeks. The feedback I have had has been massively positive. Some humbling stories of how this book has helped people.

I wanted to do a little more for those that are hugely struggling at the moment. This is where this workbook comes in. I want to give you the most simple way possible to guide you out of crippling anxiety. I have been there. I don't want you to suffer anymore.

I have kept the backbone of this book from the original. However, I have added, elaborated, changed and improved to keep it fresh. I want this book to perfectly complement the original but also can standalone too. Some things need repeating, but I don't want to make this boring.

I want to add a lot more learnings over the last two years.

When you start this book it will start with how you are feeling at the moment. Split into five categories and go through what your beliefs are. Please do not skip. It is a great temperature check on where you are at in this moment. I want you to see tangible progress in your battle with your inner drama queen.

Be prepared to lean on the edge of your comfort zone. Your new default setting!

You will see life differently. Change is coming for the good. BUT! Your anxiety won't like that! It will push back hard! It will pull out everything; all your worries, insecurities and deepest darkest fears to put you back in to its control. You will feel uncomfortable. Your anxiety will get worse. I am sorry to say, but the key to this will be your inner resilience and hope. It will get better. As you see all the drama and histrionics, all the worse case scenarios, you see that nothing happened! That your anxiety is a liar! That you will find its hold slowly but powerfully slipping. *Anxiety, you can shout, scream, bully and lie but, it's cool. I will do this anyway because you can't control me anymore!*

Your key to making your escape is how you manage yourself when anxiety kicks back and you feel uncomfortable. It's not a nice feeling leaning on your edge to start. The best way to cope before you lean in is to find inner calm and solace. By mediation or getting calm.

In previous books I have stated that when I feel fear the most, that is my gauge for where I should be heading and nothing will stop me from that path.

If that worries you too much, if the fear stops you and you don't want to do this, then I would recommend that you get another book to read. It will get uncomfortable. That's good. By pushing back is the only way you will grow and develop.

Because breaking this will be painful but ultimately rewarding. You can do it. I have, and I am an average Joe. I haven't given up, and neither should you. YOU WILL do this!

Still here! Awesome! Then I have so much I want to guide, teach and help you with! I am so excited to see your journey and life unfold before you. You will break free, you will be better, stronger and happier! Excited?

We will go through how to deal and manage with your new default setting!

I will make this as simple and easy to action as possible.

How this book is laid out.

I dedicate each chapter to you FEELING better than the last chapter. I have written it so you can describe how you want to feel by the end of each chapter. What your hopes and expectations are. I have cut back quite a lot of the book. As I wanted it even simpler and easier to follow. I have removed several chapters from *Hope over Anxiety* and merged them into different chapters. You go through each one gaining insight and knowledge before going into the next.

I have given you thought-provoking questions. Words of encouragement and ways to see challenge differently. I have removed the 'in a nutshell' at the end of the chapter and have instead replaced it with a 'don't forget', keeping your mind fresh and primed for the next chapter.

I am here to coach you. I hope this book is like me being by your side willing you on. Asking you questions that make you think and inspire you. Believing in you when you don't believe in yourself.

My pain, experiences and feelings are in every page of this book. I have found this the most challenging book I have written because I have poured, thought over, spent hours thinking on each question to ensure that I am giving you the best chance of breaking free of anxiety. It is important that this helps your life. That you can see what is possible. That you break free of the pain!

I have written from my experiences, thoughts and feelings on what being free of anxiety feels like. I hope it inspires you to see the endgame. The place you want to be. So you have something to aspire. Few describe what being anxiety free feels like. I want to show that to you. It may be different for you but at least you have something to see. What good looks like.

I have left several of the poems from the original. However, I have added several more to inspire you.

You will need a plan — don't worry, I have that covered. I will give you all that you need to guide you.

Are you excited for you to get going?

Fantastic!

Then let's begin!

Chris
January 2019

How do you feel right now?

On a scale of one to ten?

One feeling awful to ten feeling on top of the world! Rate how you feel on the following topics.

Find somewhere to record this. Keep it with you. These five points are the key to you feeling better. Focusing on them will help you. Seeing your score now and if you follow this workbook, you will feel considerably better by the end.

I will put these same questions at the back. Showing you tangible progress.

Calm
Panic
Worry
Happiness
Confidence

Beliefs

This is a little different. Rather than doing a scale of 1 to 10. I want you to put whether you feel it's true or false next to the statement.

- I feel like a victim. Everything is my fault!
- What is wrong with me?
- I don't deserve the best life possible.

- I can't handle failure.
- I can handle rejection.
- I can't take criticism.
- If I work at it, I can have what I want.
- I am good enough.
- Life is too hard.
- Anxiety is too hard. I can't break it!
- Everyone hates me!

Keep this for your records. You will need this at the end of the book.

The middle of the beginning.
My descent into the darkness
and the battle upwards.

The biggest obstacle you will ever overcome is your mind.
If you overcome that, you can overcome anything'
—Marcandangel

What is this chapter about?

This is my story of my descent to the lowest point of my life.

How I got there. What I did to slowly, fingernail by fingernail, claw my way out of the abyss.

What experiences I have had that have shaped my life up to this point.

What steps I put in place to keep growing, and my determination not to go back!

My Story—My Journey

My journey starts in the middle of the realisation that I was broken. I was suffering before this, but I hadn't realised how bad I felt. I needed this awful moment to shake me up. To see where my life was heading. It was a life changing moment.

13

12 December 2014 5.55am—My Story

It was dark, almost pitch black as I walked to my work; my convenience store that fateful day, but something felt different, something felt wrong. A part of me was screaming *'go home, go back home!'* I squashed the feeling as I opened the store and entered the premises. The alarm went off as it always did. Then it happened. He came at me, attacked me and demanded I opened the safe. I was the victim of an armed robbery. I remember shouting loudly *'oh for f**k sake'* as he entered the building, pushing me through the shop towards the safe. This was the only time I showed any negative emotions.

My life was worth £3,500!

He threatened me! Thinking about my wife and children during my 45-minute ordeal had a profound effect on me. I kept it together for the entire time; I was calm but assertive. I don't know where I got that stillness from!

It almost felt like I had detached myself from it. Like when I found out I lost my brother or sitting at his funeral. My emotions for that time were gone. I told myself that it was just an irate customer, nothing personal, deal with him then deal with your emotions. I told myself that my family depended on you. Your kids won't be without their father! My wife without her husband. It is down to you to make sure that doesn't happen.

He wanted the contents of the safe; my life depended on me opening that safe! He demanded I open it even though the timer wasn't ready. He was getting panicked. All for £3,500!

Thankfully, I am still alive to tell the tale.

After the event, I watched it on closed-circuit. I was holding my hands together, almost in prayer, as I spoke to the robber. I tried to keep him calm and manage the situation the best I could.

They left me physically okay (although I was shaking), but the mental damage was only just beginning.

I organised and got things sorted to reopen the shop. The police sent me home. They could see I was showing signs of shock.

My journey . . . into the abyss.

Over the course of the next few days, I slipped more and more into despair. Being at home on my own wasn't good for me. Too much time to think . . .

The previous six years hadn't been good; money worries, my marriage was struggling, and my job wasn't great, but this massive event was the last straw as my nerves took over. That violation had broken me. I was lost before this, but that act destroyed me. I lost what little confidence I had. I lost my strength. I lost.

Facing the person in the mirror.

I didn't like the person I had become. I felt I had become too selfish, too self-centred, too shut off to my pain and less caring of others; something in the past I felt I was good at.

Moments of fear and anger would wash over me for no reason. On regular occasions during the day, it would ambush me and take complete control.

I struggled to get out of bed. It was a huge effort. The worry about him coming back and getting into my house invaded my thoughts. I would stay up late at night watching programmes on TV—nothing I can remember; anything to take my mind away from what I was feeling. To get lost in the show and to escape my emotions. To feel something other than pain.

I would dream of a man faceless in black clothing (unrecognisable apart from a black silhouette). He would be up against our back window door and opening it to come in, with a hammer in his hand. The feelings of horror, sheer terror and impending death still scare me today and would take hours to shake off after I would wake up.

Other times I would shake with worry. All I wanted to do was curl up in a ball. Every time I looked into the mirror it would hit me. Especially on my own at night, struggling to stop weeping.

Leaving the house was difficult; it had become my fortress. Putting my feet out of the door made me very anxious. But I had to take my children to school; I had to pick them up. There was no choice in my eyes. So I battled through it.

I also felt I had to hide my pain as if I wanted to shield my wife and kids from the dark. I was also being selfish. Without saying how I felt made it less real.

My little dog laying by my side resting on my legs with his warm body was a massive comfort during those days. A calming influence. Being forced to look after him and his needs brought about a reach out to real life.

I hated myself; I hated what I had become, what it had done. I felt powerless; I felt ashamed. I blamed myself like I always do. *'What if I had not changed my shift that day? What if I had listened to my gut and not gone in? What if I had opened the store differently?'*

The days would blur in to the next. Some days I felt numb; other days the feeling would hit me hard.

I regularly went to see my GP, but couldn't put steps in place to sort myself out. I didn't want to take medication. I was offered by my GP several times, but I refused. I didn't know where to turn or had any drive to help myself. The thought of going on to medication scared me. The thought of the six weeks of being nervous and apprehensive before seeing an improvement just wasn't an option! More nervous and apprehensive than I was and trying to get back to work feeling like that? No chance!

There were times I felt it would be better for my wife and kids that I was no longer around. To stop being a burden, a pain to them. Sure, they would be upset, but long term it would be better for them. No one understood what I was going through. I felt isolated and alone. I wanted to die. But I couldn't do it. What drove me during the ordeal helped me now. I hadn't enough determination to even attempt to do it, let alone do it.

They would not destroy me. I will strive and do better. It was a massive f**k you to him.

That's how it started, then my outlook changed. My drive was still there, but my motivation was different. I wanted to do this for me. For my loved ones.

To face death—to realise, reflect, to understand what happened, to understand me—forced a realisation of what I needed to do. I asked myself:
What do I want out of life?
Who do I want to be? What obstacles will I face?
Where do I want to go?
What can I well?
How do I get better? I will get better!

I also felt lucky. Others have received worse experiences than me. It could have been far more horrific. I feel this life-defining moment was a gift. I had to change!

My Past

When I go back and think about it I have always been nervous and anxious, but the start for me was probably the death of my younger brother Thomas of cancer. He was just 20 months old.

I had chicken pox, and I was the first in our family to get it. What killed him was that virus as his body was fighting cancer. I blamed myself as a ten-year-old. It was my fault he died. I carried that guilt and pain through my childhood right the way through to my adult life. Feelings of not deserving to be happy, not feeling well enough, deserving all the pain I had. I was prone to self-sabotage even if things were going well.

Getting anxious, always thinking of the worst thing that can happen. At such an early age, life showed me the worst thing can happen. I loved him so much. Nothing made me happier than building things with cardboard boxes and sticky tape. We would play for hours in our made up cars. He had his eye removed and had a beautifully made glass one. Seeing the back of his eye wasn't a good experience for me; it was red when he didn't have the glass looking eye. He had a plastic cover instead, and to this day I can't look at people touching their eyes.

I remember going back to school after his death. The world felt different after, sadder, darker. It was as if the colour had drained out of my world. I lost my spark.

I still remember coming home from school, one day, to hearing my mum crying, wailing, squeezing his green Babygrow tight for dear life. I still hear her cry, that yearning, that pain. It haunts me. It reminds me my innocence went when he died. Feeling that pain made it worse because there was nothing I could do to mend the hole in her heart. Nothing I could have done to help her.

When we went to visit him, our last goodbye, I looked at his face and body. He looked wafer thin, unrecognisable from the boy I had seen a week previous. I noted the back of his head had been cut where they had done the autopsy. His face and body had a greyish yellow look to it. He looked unrecognisable to the brother we left when the ambulance came and picked him up. What shocked me most was the cold, ice cold feeling I felt when I touched his face. It shot straight

18

through me like a lightning bolt. So cold I couldn't touch him again. He looked so peaceful, but I couldn't face touching my brother. I regret never touching him again. I knew at the time I wouldn't have time to say goodbye. Just couldn't do it.

In Thomas' coffin, he had his yellow cuddles and his favourite teddy bear resting in between his legs. He was such a live wire, nothing fazed him. Full of energy, so fun-loving.

Some not fond memories.

I hated school. I used to travel to school by bus. One girl a year younger than me, would pin me up against the window with my back held in place. She would take great delight with a big selection of the top of the bus egging her on. My tiny frame was powerless to stop her. Pinned, unable to move, rubbing her boobs on me. She loved humiliating me in front of the others. She got a big kick out of her efforts.

When we went to an adventure week at school, one lad took great joy in picking on people. I was not very developed at school. He, with friends, pinned me and pulled my trousers down in front of many kids. They all laughed and it to this day it fills me with shame.

When I was 15, I had a chance of doing well at school and getting my grades for GCSEs, but I couldn't. I freaked out; I struggled. I was so worried I would fail, I couldn't revise. I would spend hours upstairs doing everything but revise. I hadn't the strength to do it.

At 22, I got mugged on a pub crawl. I got led to a park, talking about getting stoned together. I knew I was in trouble as they escorted me down. They held my hands behind my back as one hit me then they threw me into a tree head first with my hands still held. They demanded my Walkman, pulling a knife and demanding I give them my 21st birthday watch. I refused. I tossed my headphones at them and legged it, jumping over a brook, and off into the safety of people. I don't know where I got the speed of thought and pace from. I was too quick for them. I still don't know to this day how I jumped that brook, but I did.

My chin had swollen up. I looked like I took the full force of the tree on my chin.

I have always been anxious. I have tried to hide it—from biting my nails to using my smartphone as a safety blanket. I had found that it had kept me calmer, less worried, less anxious. But it also shut me off from life— an amazing life and people I have around me.

I may seem calm on the outside, but I am constantly worrying inside. Checking myself, making sure.

Meanwhile . . . the struggle forward.

I got a new job. I will never know how on earth I got through two interviews in the space of a few hours—my anxiety and worry was in overdrive! How on earth I kept it all in I still don't know. All I know is I felt a complete mess! Exhausted.

I went to work, but I wasn't better. I faked it. Putting on my best fake smile. I had to go back to work; we had to financially. That was the pressure I put on myself. I needed to get away from that place. From the memories.

It was back at my new job I pieced myself back together. Little by little. In some ways, it was like starting again at life. Rebuilding. I was determined that this would not break me. I was determined to do better. I had another chance! Out of all of it, I could make this a massive positive.

To strive to be the person I know I can be. Someone to be proud of.

It was a struggle. I was constantly feeling paranoid and worried. I would be sacked, thinking I would be backstabbed by my colleagues, as my trust in humanity gone. Wanting to go home, back to the security of my home. I felt isolated and alone. *Nobody wants you here, you can't do this. You aren't good enough! You are a failure. They will betray you and you will deserve it.* I distanced myself from everyone. Fear of being a failure was constantly on my shoulder.

I watched YouTube videos about believing in yourself to rebuild my confidence. I would watch inspiring upbeat clips to help me face the day.

I would look in the mirror, repeat my mantras in my head in the morning, or if I only had a few seconds, I would say *'keep doing better!'*

I started and continue to listen to superhero music to motivate me and make me feel superhuman. I do this most days first thing in the morning. I enjoy the music, but it also helps me to feel inspired and positive.

I then went further. I planned. Giving myself goals to achieve. Firstly planning, then I wrote it all down. Having goals from zero to twenty years. Things I will achieve, big dreams. Dreams I will achieve in my lifetime.

I knew it would take time, little footsteps every day.

I read a lot now, loads of self-help books. 'The Gift of Imperfection' by Brene Brown. She taught me to have barriers, what I feel I find acceptable to yourself and to show my vulnerability.

Inspiring books like 'Jobs' by Walter Isaacson and 'The '4-hour Workweek' by Timothy Ferriss to name a few, it drives my wife to distraction! It was reading Walter Isaacson's book about Steve Jobs (the man behind the iPod, iPhone and Mac) that busted open my world. Made me look up at the stars and dream of something greater. A flawed but a brilliant man believed he could do anything! He didn't understand 'no' and believed anything was possible. *Wow! This man!*

His team changed so much! What am I doing to make a difference in the world? He had no barriers! What can I do? What have I got? How can I make a difference to people? What are my skills? What experiences can I draw from?' This led me on to writing a book. I want to make a difference to others. I want to reveal my soul so it can inspire others to seek solace and hope.

Why have I done this?

I have done it so I can be a better father. I can be a better husband. So I can be better. I want to give you, the reader, hope and dreams of a grand future. I am also making up for lost time. So much time wasted on things that really didn't matter. I massively regret the paths I took. This I use now to keep me motivated.

Over the last two years, I worked hard to improve myself. I have challenged myself to improve one percent every day.

I have done this because I want to make a difference to other people; I want to make this terrible experience into something that will help others.

'Life isn't all sunshine and rainbows . . .
nothing hits harder than life'
—Rocky Balboa

It has helped me to reconnect and understand myself, accept myself more now than I ever did. It's okay not to be okay.

I have a journal I review. It reminds me how far I have come, but also I have planned what I want to do. I am not finished yet what I want to achieve in this life!

This is only the beginning!

What will get in your way?

When you start your battle to really take your anxiety on you need to be prepared. I want you to write what mind talk, worries, fears and obstacles you think might derail towards your aim: Being free of anxiety!

Once you have done this, I want you to write what you can do so you can manage the situation if these problems arise. This isn't about you worrying about them turning up. This is about you being armed and ready when they do.

What will your mind be saying to you as you improve and break free?

What tools do you think you might need or use to help you with that?

What worries do you have that could derail you?

How will you combat that?

How can you practice self-care?

What inspiring words can you use every day to keep yourself
motivated?
(I repeat this question again later.)

How can you keep going when you feel you can't?

What's the biggest thing you are excited about when you break anxiety?

How I felt after the armed robbery.

The Mirror

Have you ever struggled to look at yourself in the mirror?

To raise your head even to catch a glimpse?

To be petrified to hold that gaze of the person staring back at you?

The broken shell with no soul?

To know if you held that gaze you could not stop the tears, the cry of a person bereft of hope. Never wanting to stop crying?

Torturing themselves for everything they have done, all the failures, all the mistakes?

For all the abuse and hurt they have endured in their life, wanting no more. Wanting out?

For already feeling dead. Living each day in Hell.

Living for the days when you felt nothing.

For wanting to smash everything to pieces.

To want to punch the walls so hard that you broke your hands, covered in blood. To feel a comfort in that thought.

To want a release, anything to take back control.

For feeling shame. Like I brought it all on myself.

For feeling shame, wanting to release my anger.

For feeling shame, for not wanting anyone to see me like this. Not wanting it to affect my wife and children.

For hiding all my pain from all that love me.

The mirror doesn't lie. He sees you. He knows what you are thinking. That's why I can no longer look at it.

The Silence

All lights are out.
The darkness envelops me.
I lay here unable to speak, unable to move.
There is not a sound.
I want to cry but no tears can break free.
I want to scream, loud so loud at the top of my lungs,
ahhhhhhhhhhhhhhh.
I want all my pain and anguish to be released.
I want this desperately but no words come out.
Instead, I lay here trapped motionless, powerless, and unable to do
anything but hear the silence.

Free ME!

What does it need to take?
How hard do I need to push?
How much pain and suffering do I need to put myself to be anxiety
free?
What is the cost? My friends and loved ones? Too much pain! Too
much suffering!
Why do I keep failing?
I am such a failure! I will never do this. It hurts too much. Please
someone takes pity on me and free me!
Get me out of this hole.
SOMEONE PLEASE FREE ME!
I need saving!
I can't do this on my own!

What Is Anxiety?

*'You are braver than you believe, stronger
than you seem, and smarter than you think'*
—A.A Milne

What is in this chapter?

I will explain to you the basics of what anxiety is. What types of anxiety you can have. Some causes of anxiety and some basic ways of reducing your battles. It will give you an insight in to what I struggle with.

What is anxiety?

Everyone has anxiety in one form or another during their life. From being anxious about a job interview, exam or medical test. These are normal emotional states.

It is when we struggle to control these worries it then affects our daily lives. For me and many I have encountered, it's like a downward ever more challenging spiral.

What does your anxiety feel like?

What would you like to feel at the end of this chapter?

You can't escape anxiety once it finds you.

I have general anxiety. I find myself being irritable a lot. I find this so frustrating, and it chips away at my confidence. There are times I feel powerless, a prisoner to my emotions. I want to be a more fun-loving, calm and confident human being.

According to WebMD, general anxiety or GAD is 'Characterised by excessive, exaggerated anxiety and worry about everyday life events with no obvious reason for worry.'

Take a recent example. I was driving to a meeting. It was raining, then I heard this high -pitched sound coming from my car. *What was that? There it was again! It was going in a cycle.*

I was panicking. *I have got to get off the motorway and find out. It could be the wheel slowly falling off! Christ, how quickly will that happen? I need to slow down because if it does and I am doing 70, then I am going to be killed. That would be awful for my family. But there aren't any junctions, oh god! What am I going to do?* Each time I heard it the more I panicked and could not think. I was trying not to have an anxiety attack. I had knots in my stomach; I was trying to calm myself through breathing and self-talk, but I was struggling. I could feel my heart throwing itself into my rib cage. *Sh*t, sh*t, SH*TTT. What do I do now?* It was then I realised it was my windscreen wipers squeaking as it had stopped raining! I felt a wave of relief. I felt stupid for even panicking. But that is my mind, always looking at the impending catastrophe.

I struggle with anything outside my comfort zone or out of my norm. I procrastinate or stick my head in the sand and don't do it. The struggle to achieve is a massive battle. This has cost me so much in my life. So many times. Doing the same thing. I can't do it. It's like having to climb a huge mountain. The constant invasive depressing mind talk.

I had an anxiety attack worrying about a promotion. I had bought my son a keyboard, for my sins. The music was blaring, my son singing away, trying to get dinner organised, and my wife talking. The noise in my head and in the house was unbearable. It snuck up on me and smacked me in the face. I couldn't control it.

I had a tightening in my chest and knots in my stomach. I felt like someone had taken the wind out of me. It was my first anxiety attack for months.

People With Anxiety

When I have spoken to people with anxiety, I am amazed how many on the surface you would not expect to have it. How many people control it and appear on the outside at least like they are not dealing with anything.

Anxiety has three sides; mental, physical and emotional. Our self-talk is of worry for the future. Emotionally we feel fearful. Physically we are tense.

Fascinating fact—over 70 percent of your body's systems are used during your anxiety disorder! This explains why you always feel exhausted!

The most common symptoms can be:

- Headaches/pressure—feels like head about to explode
- Palpitations
- Dizziness
- Weak legs-feel like jelly
- Feeling detached from the world
- Tension and muscle aches
- Sweating
- Shortness of breath
- Fatigue and tiredness
- Increased heart rate
- Digestive problems
- Irritable
- Mind constantly racing

What are your anxiety symptoms? Are they similar to the ones listed or are they different?
Write here what you experience. No judgement.

This can manifest in a variety of other disorders like:

- Phobias
- Panic disorders
- Post-traumatic disorder
- Social anxiety disorder
- OCD

So many people these days suffer from one form or another. I used to live being stressed every day. It isn't healthy and burns you out. It also leads to being anxious.

Anxiety is an isolating experience. It's overwhelming. It can damage relationships with family and friends and can threaten people's careers and lives. Many people don't understand how hard and energy-sapping being anxious is.

Anxiety is so complex and individual to that person. There is a lot of different anxiety like:

Social anxiety–described by NHS.GOV as *'overwhelming anxiety and excessive self-consciousness in everyday social situations'* . . .

General anxiety (GAD)–*'Anxiety disorder characterised by chronic anxiety, exaggerated worry, and tension, even when there is little or nothing to provoke it'* .(NHS.GOV)

High-performing anxiety—*High achieving and perfectionist, driven by details and order to calm racing thoughts, worry, and the fear that invade every ounce of the mind and body'* . . . (Headspace.com)

What anxiety do you have?

People can appear to look calm, self-assured, and confident on the outside, but drowning on the inside.

There is no reasoning or logic that can help. Anxiety is purely an emotional state. Most of the time we know what is happening, we understand the logic and battle it, but we feel we have no control over what is happening.

I took four weeks just to take rubbish to the local recycling depot. The thought of going made me anxious and fraught with worry. My stomach was in knots. It has been one of the few times I couldn't explain why and still don't. I have done it loads of times in the past without problems. This time was different. I had to push myself so hard just to get it done I did it. It only took me 14 minutes to do it. Round trip. I had to listen to Marvel music to inspire me the whole time. Five bags of rubbish!

I felt stupid and ashamed afterward. *Why the hell did it take you that long? It's only just down the bloody road, you d**k!'*

There are days with this book when I have struggled to write—not due to time or other commitments but the nervousness and worry that comes with it.

Is this book going to bore people? This book has to be a beautiful piece of work, it has to! What happens if it isn't? Am I telling them the wrong information? Is this book a clever concept or total crap? Will people ridicule me for showing what my innermost fears and thoughts are? Will it affect my professional career, my children?

Days have been safer not to write. But I want to make a difference to people. The only way I will is by giving everything. And pushing beyond my fears. To show you exactly what is going on in my head.

What can cause anxiety?

Life events —This could be one major event (like me), death, car accidents, for example, or a series of stressful events experiencing many pressures all at once—relationship problems, work pressures, and financial problems. I have had all the above.

Self-talk—being on constant guard for the worst-case scenario to happen. Thinking all the things that could go wrong will prepare you for when it does.

Biological reasons—It is believed that if someone else in your family is anxious, you will have similar personality traits. I have family that struggle with anxiety.

Evolutionary reasons—Anxiety is an unpleasant experience, but it has also been important for our human evolution. When we feel in danger, our body reacts—our heart beats faster to help supply our blood to our muscles quickly, ready for us to fight or run away from dangers. We sweat to cool us down rapidly for a quick response. Both these symptoms are common in anxiety.

Who gets anxiety?

Fact - One in 10 people suffer from anxiety in one form or another during their life.

According to NHS.UK, women are twice as likely to suffer anxiety than men.

In my humble view, a lot of men aren't so willing to be forthcoming about what they have to deal with. There is feeling, especially amongst my generation, that men should not be so open with their feelings or show failings.

The truth is anyone can, from famous actors, politicians (some of the most famous of all time) to the person in the street. It does not discriminate. It does not let go once it finds you!

Anyone can get anxiety.

So many people have experienced it. I read that anxiety is having your own drama queen stuck in your head. It is an excellent and amusing description of what anxiety is like. It's your best friend knowing everything about your deepest, darkest fears and exploiting and manipulating you. Telling you aren't good enough, you're a failure, you are useless and no one likes you.

The Anxiety Stigma

So many people have anxiety, but the view can be so warped. I don't get why people can say things like: *'pull yourself together,' 'it's not that bad,' 'it's all in your head,' 'Don't be such a drama queen.'*

What people don't get is that your old part of the brain that senses threats is activated two seconds before your new part of the brain is aware (this deals with rational thought etc), meaning you can't control the anxiety. It's already there before you control it!

It's real. It can be exhausting and soul destroying. I never asked for this; I never wanted it. I have maximum respect for those that deal with it every day. I am lucky; I know many other people who have worse anxiety than I do.

Ways of Reducing Anxiety

Here are a few examples—we will discuss a lot more in future chapters.

- Get a routine.
- Schedule things.
- Exercise is more effective than controlling your anxiety.
- Be creative, so writing a book, drawing, etc has also been suggested to help.
- Mindfulness.

Some Basics

Below is a list of the basics you can focus on helping improve your anxiety. A lot of these are easier said than done:

- Understand yourself.
- Learn more about anxiety—having the knowledge is the first step.

- Learn to challenge your unhelpful thoughts. Try to see things in a more balanced light. I use meditation for this. But sometimes it is still difficult.
- Improve your problem-solving skills.
- Learning and reducing your time spent worrying.
- Learning ways to be relaxed.
- Learning methods to prevent you from avoiding anything that makes you feel anxious—procrastination my good friend.

You don't cure anxiety. Being anxious has an important part to play in your life, you need it.

We can learn to find ways of understanding your anxiety. Managing anxiety is your best way to deal with it. Fighting head on, trying to control it is probably the worst thing to do.

When you make changes at the start, it will get harder, up to now you have been just coping with it. The long-term benefits though are more than worth it. To break the cycle needs something different.

Each one of us is different and individual. It is your own needs and the best ways for you that will make a difference. In this book, I will help with that.

A few questions to consider:

What makes you anxious?

How do you think?

What do you say to yourself?

How do you feel?

What are the physical symptoms for you?

Don't Forget!

- Anyone can get anxiety. It doesn't discriminate.
- What anxiety do you have? Knowledge is power. You can arm yourself if you know what you have.
- There are many ways that can help you with your anxiety. We will talk more about this throughout the book. So don't worry. You will not need to worry about it all now! Getting calm, having a structure, and being happy are the three most important!

I will not lose this war!

I feel pain and struggle, there is a weight on my back too much for one person to carry.

I feel shame, sadness and tremendous loneliness.

But there is a fire burning in my belly, a passion, and a will I have never felt before.

NO MORE! Will I feel like this!

NO MORE! Will my self-pity, worry, fear and sadness be what controls me!

NO MORE! Will I accept the old standard. I am going forward, I will be the person I know I can become! I am stronger, I know what I can be!

I know how I can break free.

I know that each day will be a battle, but I will not cross that line. I will not go back. I will NOT surrender. It will take all I have. It will cost me. But it will be rewarding.

And there is nothing my anxiety can do that will stop me!

Enough! You are done controlling my life!

Enough! I am stronger! I will beat you!

My Mantras—My Daily Affirmations

My mantras, I feel them. When I say them to myself. I get strength, courage and heart from saying these every day. Some days are more difficult than others.

'I will face a fear.'

'My best is good enough.'

'I can't do everything in one day, but I can take one small step.'

'I will stop and smell my roses.'

'Be a somebody that makes everyone feel like a somebody.'

My Domian.com

What are your mantras?

What inspires you and fills you with hope?

What are your values?

For you to be anxiety free you need to know who you are, what you will tolerate and have clarity on your future. Sounds easy right?

This is to help you stay focused, to understand what is important to you and remind yourself who you are. This exercise is so much more than putting a few words on a page. It is who you want to become. So don't skip it. Invest the time in getting this done. When you are done you will have a clear focus on who you are. I have found with clarity in who you are has built my confidence and reduced my anxiety.

Start off listing 25 values you have. List them here.

Some examples below.

Please list more that you feel are important to you:

Love
Joy
Happiness
Kind
Loving

Now cut these down to five — Yep FIVE. Tough, huh?

Okay, let's go even further. Get down to three.

Mine have changed to these three. I have got them from Brendan Burchard. They really rang true. The most important one is: matter. I need to make sure that every day that I have helped someone else. That I matter.

Ask yourself...

Have I...... today with all three of your values. If you don't know or you are unsure with what you are doing, how things are going or how you are behaving ask...your three values. If they aren't part of it, then don't do it.

Live,
Love,
Matter.

I ask myself every night before I go to bed, and I record the details. I hold my three core values up. That is the light. I head towards. I want to live passionately, be present with everyone. Love with all my heart, be vulnerable and make a bloody difference to people.

If you don't achieve what you wanted today, that's okay. It isn't a stick to beat yourself with. Instead, record how you will do better tomorrow. How you want to behave and be.

What are your triggers?

'Anxiety does not empty tomorrow of its sorrows,
but only empties today of its strength.'
—Charles Spurgeon

How do you want to feel after you have completed this chapter?

My aim for you, my hope, is that you can see what your triggers are with anxiety. You have a clear path on what to do. We will ask questions that will challenge you. I expect you are frank and honest, with yourself. That you don't hold back. Remember, you are the only person that will see what you write. What your words say and mean are all for you.

My first question of this chapter is simple. How do you want to feel at the end? What is the clear hope? What's the ideal outcome?

Write it down and focus on getting exactly what you want from it. The importance is that you are clear and in control. This is all about you.

Write It Here.

Get Calm

Before we ask some challenging questions that could trigger worry, nervousness and even a panic attack, I highly recommend listening some inspiring beautiful music or meditation. I have a breakout chapter later in the book. Feel secure, comfortable and calm so that your brain is in the logical and analytical side. My hope is you feel happy to record your feelings and excited to learn what is triggering your fears.

Imagine how knowing what your anxiety is doing. What your triggers will do for you. Feel it, experience the empowerment. Explain in your own words what it will feel like. Allow the feelings of hope come to the surface.

Write here what you hope to feel.

Your Anxiety — My Anxiety Attacks

My physical symptoms—I slur my words, lose words completely. I physically shake, overcome with fear.

46

I can get petty about silly things. It has to be that way. That's my preference, do what I ask. Everything has to be that way. Don't argue, just do it!

Fast-talking, stuttering, stumbling over words. Or losing a word completely. I am mortified as I stumble further. Then I try to think of the word, and I only feel more anxious and embarrassed. More words fail me. I feel on show I want to disappear. I feel stupid. This is when I have to do something I am not prepared for. If I must talk in front of others or if I feel self-conscious.

Going quiet, zoning out and sitting rigid—this has happened a few times. When I was under the most stress. This is me at my worst. I have had this mainly at work. I can't stop them; they come over me. I feel paralysed. I witness the whole thing, it's scary as hell!

Memory loss—getting things jumbled up. My short-term memory is bad at the best of times, but when I am most stressed, and my anxiety kicks in, I lose important conversations. I can't repeat anything that happened, despite listening the whole time—even things that happened only five minutes ago.

These were my struggles. Record here your physical symptoms when you have a panic or anxiety attack.

The most important part of your triggers is understanding what they are. The emotional struggles. The things you know kick off your anxiety.

I shall give a few examples. But watch them over the next few weeks and discover them.

I would highly recommend that you write on a scale of one to ten the following: one being rarely worry, to ten being full-blown panic. Then add other ones. This isn't an exclusive list. There may be others that may be more important to you.

Once you have listed them on a scale. You can then analyse what your triggers are! Cool, I think. These are then the areas you can work on:

- Death.
- Being bullied.
- Shouted at.
- Leaving the home.
- Getting close to someone.
- Being able to say you need help.
- Feeling useless.
- Feeling a failure.
- What effects do your triggers have on you?

We have discussed the physical symptoms. But this is the mental feelings.

What do you feel when you have an attack?

What do your thoughts say?

What do you wish you could feel instead?

Looking after yourself.

This is a big thing with us anxiety sufferers. If you are to break free, be kind and considerate to yourself. Remove the high expectations and the constant overthinking and analyzing of yourself and situations.

A Pledge

I want you to sign down here how you will do things differently from now on. How you will be determined getting enough sleep and how you can be kind and considerate as possible. Treat yourself like your best friend.

I _____

declare that I will no longer accept the old me. I know what my triggers are and resolve to fix them. One by one. I will look after myself, being kind and loving to what I am doing. I will constantly reflect on my progress and be proud of the person I am becoming. I rock!

Signed _____

Dated _____

When In A Panic Attack — What You Should Do!

Now you know your physical symptoms. Breathe deeply and slowly. Raise your eyes in to a soft focus, not looking at anything. Understand that it will only last maximum 20 minutes. Say *'it's okay, this is me when I am having a panic attack.'* Note your physical symptoms. How is my breath? When the shame and panic come ask yourself '*is this true?*' Breathe through it. You will get panic attacks, and that's okay. It will take time to improve. But you will. The key is to breathe through it. Don't resist it.

Don't forget!

- What are your physical symptoms?
- Visualise what you want from this. How it feels to have control and understanding over your triggers?
- Understand your triggers. So you can take them on and fix them.

Building Your Self-Confidence

*'If you don't have confidence, you will
always find a way not to win.'*
—*Carl Lewis*

How do you want to feel after you've completed this chapter?

To get your mind thinking. You can use what I have written below or you can do something that may feel more personal to you.

'I feel hope. I feel empowered. I know I will have battles and struggles, but that's okay. I will make mistakes, but that's okay too. I feel in control. I feel a happiness in myself. I feel I want to share my joy to others. I have this iron will. I will be successful because I believe in who I am. No one needs to tell me I am a good person because I feel it.'

Write here what YOU want to feel.

What Is Self-Confidence?

Understanding what you are good at. Having a belief in yourself and how you convey this to others. You can learn self-confidence and you can grow it. It's a skill.

Self-confidence is the KEY to breaking anxiety. EVERYthing stems from building your self-confidence. Watch your anxiety. See what it says. It will undermine your belief in yourself. Stopping you from breaking out of your box. The more self-confidence, the quieter anxiety gets.

How does it feel?

It's like having sunshine on the inside. That nothing can faze you. You feel good about yourself.

How do you want to feel when full of self-confidence?

Write it here. Be honest and emotional. Really feel it. Allow the feelings to course through your veins.

What do I need to do to find ways of building self-confidence?

Set up a journal or diary or even a notepad! They are relatively cheap.

Record what you are doing and experiencing. With each new experience of doing something you love or learning on the edge of your comfort zone, you become happier and more self-confident.

Each time you feel low and don't think you can do this reread your experiences. What you have done up to this point. You will find yourself feeling inspired, full of motivation and proud of your progress.

Find some motivational music (talked about later in this workbook). Motivational inspiring videos or words of encouragement.

Ways of building YOUR self-confidence.

Using *Hope over Anxiety* book as a guide. I want you to pledge here: Haven't got the book? Click the link <u>here</u>!

I pledge to treat myself like I would my closest and dearest friend. I will be kind and considerate. Pick me up when I am down. Encourage and help myself. But most of all, I will show complete love for myself. I am doing my bloody best. I am getting better, but I need to time to grow. I need to give myself a pat on the back every so often, and I need to not give myself such a hard time. I didn't ask for this. I will break free but with compassion, love and heart. Not with anger, frustration and aggression. That's how anxiety rolls. I don't.

Signed _____

'The hardest step she ever took was
to blindly trust in who she was.'
—Atticus

Additional how to lean on to the edge of the comfort zone.

I have already said in this book that should be your new default setting. It will be your quickest way of building your confidence. Pushing back your anxiety and keeping it there! Pushing the walls of your comfort zone. What your challenge is to manage your anxiety doing this. There will be times when you will not get this right, and you will fall back. Struggling to sleep, feeling that anxiety is coming back tenfold but— and it's a huge BUT— don't fall back! Don't give up. Keep going. Note why you got it wrong and resolve to fix it.

When you have got it right, that's the kicker! When you do, you will feel on the top of the world!

More evidence to prove that your are bloody great!

By managing how you are feeling, by using tools in your swag bag, you can deal with that uncomfortable feeling. The anxiety and worry can be managed over time.

How do you want to feel on the edge of your comfort zone?

Breathe in deeply and out slowly and write a positive view of how YOU want to feel when you are taking on your fears. It should be like you are atop of a mountain looking ahead at this amazing view.

Make it as emotional as possible.
Write it here…

You need to have a structure to your day. It details this in Freedom over Anxiety and a little here. Making sure you are calm and in control. So that when a trigger goes off, you are in a good place to manage the situation. As you get more confident, this will become much easier. I have gone over two years now WITHOUT a panic attack, so I know what I am talking about.

Tools Needed/Hints and Tips

- Slow and deep breathing. Box breathing — breath in for a count of five. Hold for five. Then breathe out for a count of five.

- Watch your thoughts. Write here what your thoughts are saying!
- Don't judge yourself. They are just thoughts, chatter. Most of it is meaningless.
- Structure. At least three times a day. Get calm.
- Focus on worrying for 15 minutes a day only. The rest, enjoy your life. So when you do worry say *'I shall put that in my worry time.'*
- Appreciate what is around you.

Don't forget!

- **Self-confidence is a skill and is learned. How will it feel to have it in abundance?**
- **Anxiety will hit back when you're leaning on the edge of your comfort zone. Have tools to cope with your new default setting.**
- **Be kind and compassionate to yourself.**

My gratefulness diary and planning for the future.

'Be thankful for what you have. Your life, no matter how bad you think it is someone else's fairy-tale.'
—*Wale Ayeni*

How do you want to feel by the end of this chapter?

This is about rewiring your brain. It is writing your achievements and what you have done for the day.

It's about being clear what you want with your life. Where you want to go.

Where do you want to take your life?

What would you love to do but are too afraid to ask?

If you are not sure, use mediation get calm and quiet. Make sure there are no distractions around you. Breathe deeply but slowly. Then ask yourself: What do I really want with my life?

You may have to ask a few times. Let it sink in to you and wait for the reply. In times of struggle and lack of clarity with my life, I have paused and asked myself that question. The answer will surprise you!

Write what you want. Don't let your anxiety talk you out of setting an intent to do something about it. We ALL have big dreams. Now it's your time to head towards it. It will require courage, joy, love and the willingness to change/improve.

Set up your goals. From that answer break it up into manageable chunks.

What do you want to do?

What are your hopes and dreams?

What are your wishes?

Something fascinating that I learned is that you need people to help you reach your dreams. It has blessed me with so many people willing and wanting to help me. It has been quite a humbling experience. It has spurred me on.

Who will help you on your journey?
(Write a list of names who will help you.)

Don't forget!

- How do you want to feel when you appreciate life?
- Having clear goals will give you the challenge and drive to achieve anything you want to in life!
- Where do you want to take your life?

The Halfway Stage — Check In

How are you feeling?

Are you feeling inspired and ready to continue?

Write down how you are feeling. Describe how empowered you feel. Ready to continue in the next half of the book.

Want an extra bit of motivation?

Anxiety is tough. There are times when you have to battle to do anything. But what would happen if you could use that battle and keep going to drive to be a better you? What would it feel like if you could see yourself progressing and feeling happier? You can do this because I have been through this pain too. The other side is worth it. You want to get to a place where your anxieties are only when you are getting married or you have a new job. The stuff you should have anxiety for.

You can do this because it requires the one thing you have in spades. WILL! If you didn't have that WILL through all the pain, you wouldn't be here. Utilise that drive to get this workbook done. Read a little a day. Then implement it. This book isn't a read from cover to cover and do. This is about what you can achieve. One step every day.

Imagine

Pick up the phone and ring me. You have become anxiety free for over a year. Describe, full of emotion and excitement, what has happened to you in that year. Be wild with what's happened. Let the writing just flow. No barrier is impossible. No life cannot be lived. All it takes is WILL.

Will you chose a life full of hope?
Because I do for you!

Then send your message to me my email is
mosschristopher799@gmail.com
If you wish. I would love to hear from you!

Ruminate:

Overthink, obsess about.

Catastrophising:

Irrational thought that something is worse than actually is.

To worry or panic about the worst thing that can happen, from any circumstances.

Dictionary.com

My Hope

I remember a time when I felt I deserved nothing but pain.

I hated myself and wanted to push everyone away.

I felt guilty when things were going well.

Expecting disaster to strike or doing all I could to make it happen.

I felt a cold shell aimlessly trying to survive me. Looking for battles in all the wrong places. Expecting all my loved ones to let me down.

This is before I found hope.

I can now look up at the sky and be privileged to see the beauty in the world.

To touch a rose petal, to feel its softness and strength.

To feel the lick of the wind during a hot summer's day.

To watch with joy seeing a bird soaring, riding the sky.

To look up at the sky and see the wonder in the clouds. To be amazed.

To see the world as it should be.

To know the challenges and struggles I will face but know they will pass.

To know my anxiety will be good on some days and bad on others. To be okay with that. To know I will be anxiety free.

To know I will get better and stronger. To see how far I have come in such a short time.

To feel joy, intense, amazing and moving.

To know fear but know it will no longer hold me back.

To look in the mirror, hold my gaze and say I am okay.

To have so much love and hope for others. To want people to grow and take real joy in their happiness.

This is my hope.

This is me now.

This is my soul.

Structure

'I have cracked my rituals. It's a habit I don't have to battle to get what I need to do anymore because it's a natural thought. I enjoy getting calm and having some me time.'
— Christopher Moss

What is this chapter about?

I designed this to help you. Get your key mental health exercises into ritual. To the point so they get done. Without having to battle to do them.

I have done it so you can pick what to do. What you feel comfortable with.

How would you feel if you could have time to have a structure that will help you with your anxiety?

How do you want to feel by the end of this chapter?

I will split this into 3 parts:

Morning Rituals

This is what you do from the second you wake to breakfast. Choose one of the following (YOU can do all if you wish):

I find the best way is to slow myself down. Because my brain is in overdrive when I wake. Slowing down your breathing and mindfully watching what you do will have an excellent start to your day. Meaning less exhaustion to start it off.

- Before you leave your bed mindfully meditate; listen to inspiring meditation.
- Take the dog for a walk. Leave your phone at home and go for a walk. Even if it's around the block. Slow down your breathing. Watch the world. Look up at the sky take the world in.
- When you have your first cup of tea or coffee in the morning. Breathe slowly, let the kettle boil. Appreciate the drink, smell it. Breathe slowly.
- When you wake up ask yourself how will I enjoy myself today?
- Ask yourself how do you want to show up in the world today?

Dinner time!

The 15 minute reset. It's important that halfway through your day you stop and get calm. Allowing you to reset. To stop and slow yourself down again.

Choose ONE of the following:

- Listen to a motivational YouTube meditation.
- Listen to calm but inspiring music.
- Make a cup of coffee. Turn it into a ritual. Allow the kettle to boil. Breathe in.
- Box breathe. Remind yourself how you want to be for the rest of the day.
- If you have more time meditate for 15 minutes.

Bed time!

Hitting the sack and what you do is a key to having a good night sleep. With you choosing your structure to your day you find that your body and mind will already be in a good place.

Choose TWO of:

- Write a journal. Describe how your day has been. Find three things you loved today. Sit back and really feel the emotion of what you enjoyed. Go back in your mind. Play it over again and feel it. I love doing this!
- Write three things you appreciate today.
- Meditate. Find a calming meditation. Music is good. Slow and calming.
- Meditate. Let the day wash over you. Think of the moments of your day in 30 seconds. Like a slideshow.

What times during your day can you do your structure?

When are the best times for you to do your three morning rituals?

To do your midday rest?

To do your two sleep rituals?

Then follow them.

Don't forget!

- Structure to your day is an important step to breaking anxiety.
- What would your structure look like?
- Breaking up your day with resets — moments of calm will give you a better night sleep, reduce your anxiety and panic attack. Consistently doing this will aid you in breaking free.

Advanced training — Watching the experiencer. A place to strive to be!

Say what?

This seems like it shouldn't be here. You may look at this and be thinking. What the hell is this sh*t?! Bear with me. I will reveal all, and I am hoping by the end of it you will have a good understanding what watching the experiencer is all about.

I want to help you see what is happening to you. To watch your anxiety and mind talk. To be in a position where you can watch and NOT react!

I have put this chapter in here to get your mind thinking about what the endgame is for you. I hope most of what I write here resonates with you. Some of it may not, but it's where I wish you to get to.

What is this about?

This is getting calm and watching your thoughts. Seeing what is going on but being able to stay in control without getting pulled down into the experience. This chapter replaces ALL three of my original mindfulness chapters.

Imagine how it would feel to be empowered? Watch your thoughts come and go. Feel but not take away your happiness? Describe how that would feel to you?

Getting Calm

Describe what getting calm feels like to you?

You are not your thoughts!

I am sure you have read loads of time: you are not your thoughts. But what does that mean?

I have removed the three meditation chapters from my original book HOPE OVER ANXIETY.

Because I wanted to let you experience from my own eyes what CALM is and allowing yourself to see what is happening.

Calm is one of four cornerstones to breaking anxiety. But, I wanted to do something a little different. If you want to know more about meditation, then I would highly recommend reading *Hope over Anxiety* or *Power over Anxiety*. I have several simple techniques that can help you.

I will assume that you have read Hope over Anxiety. I want to show you what you can FEEL when you feel calm and you have meditated.

So let's cut to the chase, what on earth are you on about Chris? Watching the what? You are talking rubbish!

Let's imagine you are watching a film. You see and hear, but that's pretty much it. Even then you can get lost in it. Experiencing the events unfold. But let's say now that modern technology has seriously upgraded watching a film. Now it's not 3-D, but you can touch, feel and think the film! How often are you going to get lost in the events of the film now? How often are you going to become what's happening in the film? The experience? Can you see where I am going with this?

The life you are experiencing isn't yours. Does that make sense? You are seeing this life, but it isn't you. That's the distance you need to be. There are three parts to your brain. ALL of them are protecting you. From social situations, to feeling like you belong, to spotting threats. Your brain will pull up experiences, triggers and stories from your past to make sense of the world to protect yourself from it. And, boy, does it try to protect you. It doesn't care if you are happy. That's not its function. It merely is an overpowering older sibling.

What you want to feel.

The end goal. To be anxiety free. To have no resistance!

Life is painful. We don't have control over it. But, boy, do we resist it. Our biggest pains are when we don't accept things when we try to push our feelings down. Suppress them, deny that they are there. We fight for everything we have to control a world we can never control.

Wouldn't it be easier to accept that? To acknowledge our pains and let them pass?

To really feel it come over you but stay in the position of watching it, not getting sucked in to much. Not to protect yourself from it. But feel it all? Scary feeling right?

I am practicing it now. To ALLOW my pain and struggles to breathe, to give it space. Allowing it to sit with me. I find by doing it, it significantly reduces the time I take to deal with it by over 75 percent. In the past, some pains I have experienced have taken me months to go. I would fight like mad to hold them down, to suppress them, ignore them, not deal with them at all — sticking my head in the sand — a big one for me. But now it has gone down to days or even hours. It feels a strong emotional experience I am still getting pulled down, but I get a strong feeling of release when it goes. I can literally feel it dissipate. Almost like my brain says *'Okay, my mind is done with the pain now.'*

Do you know how empowering that feels?

How do you get to that point?

By meditating and getting calm. To watch your thoughts and feelings.

Imagine you are sitting near the top of a beautiful mountain. Close your eyes. Imagine, what does it look like? What does the sky look like? How do you feel? Looking down, you can see an endless pit. You can see, feel, taste and touch everything that comes up from the bottom. The most important thing you need to make sure you rarely get down from your amazing position. Watching all these amazing experiences both good and terrible. Letting those feelings be in you but not control you. To breathe, to see them but not let them control you.

I am not expecting you to be perfect. It will take time to allow your pain to sit with you and allow it to go. To stay as the watcher to your thoughts and feelings is challenging and will take practice, perseverance and the ability to learn and be calm. Often.

So what is actually the point to this then?

Imagine what it will feel like if you could find your soul more often? That calm, sensitive and wise person. To be able to have more energy. Be more confident, but most of all, happiness comes out of every pore?

Less energy wasted on the things that don't f**king matter.
Quicker times being in pain and struggle. Less resistance?

I don't expect you to achieve this straight off. It will take time. But you now have your end goal. A place you can take yourself. A place to strive for!

Don't forget!

- **You are in your own film. With upgraded touch, smell, thoughts and feeling. Don't get lost in the show. Using your breath and keeping calm you can see what is happening.**
- **This is an advanced practice I want to show you to inspire you to strive for!**
- **To experience feelings but not be able to get pulled away is a place I hope you can strive for.**

Obituary

'You were put on this earth to achieve your greatest self,
to live out your purpose, and to do it courageously.'
—Dr. Steve Maraboli

What is this chapter about?

Death is an absolute. It will happen to all of us. There is no getting
away from it. It is important that you appreciate what you have and
what legacy you want to leave the world.

One of my favourite films is Saving Private Ryan. It has a moment at
the end, near the end of his life.

He kneels in front of the grave to the leader that saved him during
WORLD WAR II. Weeping, his last words before he died next to him,
were simple *'Earn this, Earn it'*. Thoughts going through his head that
his life has to be special he has to be the best version of himself. Not
just for him, but for all of those that gave their lives so he could have
his.

He talks about hoping that he has had a good life. He says to his wife
'Tell me I have lived a good life. Tell me I am a good man.' It's a moving scene,
and I use it to inspire me. I am here for a reason, just like every single

one of us is. I want to earn what I have in the past taken for granted. Life, being lucky, having my health, having a loving family.

Writing your own obituary is morbid, but it is also essential to focus and give you a purpose. A life purpose. What do you want from your life? What is your purpose? What do you want to achieve? Life is so short, time is a precious commodity. I want to achieve so much. I want to make a difference to people. I want to achieve what I have set out to achieve as I am driven and determined.

At the end of Titanic when the camera pans across, all of Rose's achievements are shown. I want to make sure I have had a good life; I have completed all the goals I have set myself. Making some amazing experiences they will hold for the rest of their lives and be shared with the people I love most dearly—my long-suffering wife, my children and the rest of my family. I want to have utilised to the best of my ability, all the skills, learnings, and personality I have been given. This is a massive challenge, one I am up for. That's my ambition. That's my legacy.

My obituary if it was now . . .

We are saddened by the passing of our father and husband. His bland cooking and soul-crushing pasta bakes had even the stoic of stomachs running for cover. He passed having done a bit of stuff, not achieved much and focused too much on his job.

He was married for 17 years leaving two children.

My obituary as I want it to be . . .

We are sad to announce his passing in his sleep. Leaving his 99-year-old wife. Surrounded by his grandchildren. His list of achievements includes being a qualified counsellor. He has travelled the world. Having some amazing experiences, the chocolate-loving, storytelling, fun-loving old codger leaves a legacy. He helped so many people in his life. He gave so many experiences to his children and many fond memories.

Then drop this to just 20 words or enough you can remember and recall with ease. This is your vision, what you aspire to!

To give yourself a purpose. A reason it fires me up. I want to be the best me I can. I need to feel productive, to achieve what I want to in my life, and to make up for lost time, every moment has to count.

My 20 Words . . . My vision of what I want to be.

To inspire others, to reach out to 500,000 people. Travel the world. To be a man my family is proud of.

Now it's your turn!

Write your obituary . . .

Break it down to 20 words . . .

What are your barriers?

What is stopping you in being a better you?

Ponder for a moment you have died. What will people say about you? What do you want to say about you? What legacy do you want to leave?

This is a little morbid, but you need to think about death a lot. This will keep you focused and to remind you how short and precious life is.

What is your life purpose?

I want to make a difference to others; I want to be a husband, son, and father to be proud of.
I want to inspire others, to help them find their way out of anxiety, to push themselves beyond what they could feel possible, to be their best!
I want other people to feel comfortable, inspired, and joyful around me.
I want to push beyond—way, way beyond—my comfort zone.
I want to break my challenging goals then set up even harder ones!
I want to be the best me I can be!
I want to give my children the best life possible.
I want to give my family the best experiences I can dream of.

What is your life purpose?

What is your perfect day? What life would you love?

What I want you to consider is what it will feel like, what you would wish to be your perfect day? Something you can dream of and strive to achieve. And what is getting in the way to achieve this? Be inspired to push yourself beyond, see your dream become a reality!

Wouldn't that be amazing?

What would happen if you achieved this! Just think about that for a second.

I am sure you are reading this and saying, no chance! There is absolutely no way that this will happen. EVER! What I will say to you is this: You have come this far, daring to dream, pushing your own barriers, giving you that confidence and belief. Hope will give you the confidence to live your best life. What you dream to achieve.

It could be as simple as being able to go down to the shops and spend time with your friends.

It could be travelling to another country.

Expand this. If you can dream your perfect day, what could be the life you will love?

Consider the next few questions . . .

What will that feel like?

WHAT WILL YOU DO?

How would it feel getting up symptom free?
Imagine and write.

Imagine how you would feel about life.

Imagine what your home would look like.

Imagine what you would love to do.

Imagine what your friends would be.

Imagine how your perfect day and life would feel.

DARE TO DREAM, you might just surprise yourself!

Don't Forget!

- **Think about death and how you can make an impact to your loved ones. Not to be morbid. But to inspire you.**

Anxiety and Being Creative

'Expand your mind. Touch your pain and let all of it pour out of you. Whether it is painting, writing, drawing, or anything that helps your anxiety and your suffering be made into something beautiful. Allow you to make your suffering a joy. A creation. Moments of bliss.'
— Christopher Moss

What I want for you in this chapter?

How you can cope with anxiety by being creative. By letting your hair down. By having fun! You can pick which ones you would most like to do. Being creative is its own therapy! In it you will discover why being creative is important and how it will help you break anxiety, what your joy is and to encourage you to use it. Every day.

What do you want for this chapter?

Why be creative?

Being creative helps to reduce stress and anxiety. I like to write, but there are so many other things you can do to help. If you could feel happy at least once a day wouldn't you do it? Wouldn't you then make sure you did it? And not let anything stop you in doing it?

If you want any more ideas, then I would recommend using my first book HOPE OVER ANXIETY for inspiration.

What things can you do?

What do you love to do but don't have time or have other commitments? Maybe even you think kids do that. This shouldn't matter. What do you love to do? If it's doodling, cool. This is a preference. This gives you a sense of fun.

As we get older, we lose our sense of fun and playfulness. I encourage you to put that back into your life. You want to be your best you, you must play, have fun. It gives you so many benefits. Like a natural drop in anxiety! Feeling happier.

I have said this previously, but I will say it again. It is a simple formula:

PROGRESS = HAPPINESS.

If you aren't progressing and you can't see you are progressing, you won't be happy.

Daydreaming

Daydreaming can help you in so many ways. It can solve stressful problems, it relaxes you and inspires creativity. Doing this also helps to calm you. It has helped me come up with some ideas for my future books. Being in daydream mode is when you are in your most creative place. I highly recommend setting aside time to daydream. You will be amazed what comes out of your head!

I love to daydream. I get so many stories and I seem to look at other people's point of view, which helps, too, to keep me balanced.

Creativity is in every single one of us. Most of us never use it or get the best out of it. It allows us to develop personally and professionally, to view problems in a different way, and use different parts of our mind that previously we may not have tapped into. The confidence I have got from this has been great. Even just having that sense of fun or something to look forward to, is a help and will be to you.

When can you have 5 minutes today to daydream?
Write it down here as a commitment.

What do you love to listen to that fills your soul with joy?

Do you love to read? What do you like to read?

Getting into the zone!

When your juices are in full flow, you have got your head down and you are creating something amazing. Time stops, your mind naturally removes your anxiety and sense of time.

As you get better at what you are doing, the more times you will get into the zone. Meaning more times you will feel a natural reduction in your anxiety. Can't be bad, can it?

Describe here how you would like to feel when you are in the zone? Perhaps there has been a few experiences in the past when this has happened. That you can draw from?

Don't forget!

- Anxiety is naturally reduced when you are creative. But they need to be challenging.
- The more you are creative the more time you will get into the zone! So it's in your best interest to be creative.
- Whatever your joy is, make it a habit to do every day. Even when you are busy. Even for just 30 minutes.

Investing in You

'Investing in yourself is the best investment you will ever make. It will not only improve your life, it will improve the lives of those around you.'
—*Robin S. Sharma*

What do you want from this chapter?

Write what you want to feel like after this chapter. Do you want to feel empowered? Do you want to feel happy and delighted to see progress in your life? What do you want to feel?

Investing in yourself will give you the support and guidance you need. If you feel you need to improve your knowledge, invest in books that inspire you. Or maybe you want to improve you, invest in a life coach. It is about helping you get the best you that you can be!

What would you like to invest in?
If you can't afford it now. Make it a goal to achieve.

This investment, whether it is time or money, is never a waste. The biggest gift you can give others is your best you. As a person, we are always growing! We will never be perfect. No one is perfect!

You should always do something. I call this the one percent effect. If you do one percent improvement every day in a month, that is 30 percent better! Further away from anxiety and better as a person.

The key to ALL of this is to record how you are getting on. So you can see your own progress. Our brain 'resets' who we are and normalise where we are at. So we don't see what is happening. You can become frustrated not believing you are improving. By recording how you are feeling and what you have improved, it will give you confidence, heart and encouragement. I am GETTING better!

Take a recent example. I felt down. I didn't feel I was making any progress over the first part of 2019. Book sales weren't going anywhere, I wasn't feeling like I had progressed myself and I had done nothing. I felt that I was in a state of constant struggle.

So I went back and read my journal. My book sales are far better consistency than they have ever been. I give myself a hard time because I expect most of the time the impossible, and I am impatient. You may feel like this too. One of my biggest faults. I have read and implemented four books that month. Yes, that's right, four books, I am also dealing with pain in a different way. I used to push it away. Become protected against it. Now I let it in. Sit over it. Watching the pain. I still need to improve being able to not take it out on my family. I have done this so it can go more quickly. I feel it let all the pain go over me but it leaves me far quicker if I acknowledge it and let it in. Not to let the shutters up. 2019 was about removing the resistance from my life. Getting rid of anxiety, almost. By feeling it. I have noticed it goes so much more quickly, and I have so much more energy. I feel the release as it goes.

I am also speaking to so many more people, helping them with anxiety.

But my brain has reset all of that as the new normal. So, if I hadn't recorded these details, I would have continued to feel disheartened. Can you see why it's so important?

What would you like to do to invest in yourself?

What would you like to improve?
Be honest and remove the emotion from it.

Where would you like to take your life?

Write a list down of your strengths here—you know you have them.

Understanding how important investing in yourself is, is an imperative step in your movement away from anxiety. The investment has so much of an impact on not just you but what is possible. NEVER be afraid to improve yourself. You will find so many changes when you start. Investment in time and money. The money invested is always a great benefit to you. It could be financial, or it could be emotional.

Don't forget

- Investing in yourself isn't selfish. It is the most selfless thing you can give a person — your best self.
- They say ten percent of your money should be invested in yourself.
- Think about what you would like to improve. Who will help you on this journey? Life coaching is getting popular and is much needed. To learn skills and tools to help you and to see your own potential. We believe in you even when you don't.

Developing YOUR Hope

'Sees the invisible, feels intangible,
and achieves the impossible'
—www.Facebook.com/beyondyourself09

What is this chapter about?

Hope.The cornerstone of this book and the reason you WILL break anxiety. That feeling that despite all the pain. The struggles and the failures, you have this burning belief it will be okay. You can break free. You can do it. I have morphed the power of resistance in to this chapter too.

You have this burning desire that won't go away. You feel now is your time to shine. Whatever that has happened in the past. Your old stories. It will burn away your old negative mind from the hope you now feel.

How do you want to feel by the end of this chapter?

What do you think hope feels like?
Describe it. Add as much emotion as possible.

How do I find my hope?

Under the stairs? Left hidden in one of your children's toys?

You build it. It starts as something tiny and you allow it to blossom. Believe in the impossible! Start with determination and will to achieve, then grow it. Knowing hope is a massive factor in your change is the first step. Hope is not just an emotion but a way of thinking! It is a skill that needs to be developed.

Developing Your Hope

Having a journal also comes in very handy, helping build and grow your hope as you record your accomplishments. Building your self-confidence.

I want you to choose TWO of the following and implement them.

What two things you will do to develop, to cultivate and grow your hope? So it overpowers your anxiety? With all the other emotions that come behind that hope: happiness, drive, self-confidence — you get the picture.

- Praise yourself, celebrate your positive traits.
- Surround yourself with positive, supportive people. People that will encourage you and make you feel valued. With everything in life you can more achieve more with good people than on your own.
- Role model? Is there anyone from your friends or family you could use as an example to help in your accomplishments? Is there anyone famous that you can learn from? Are there people with a specific set of skills you can learn? If you aren't sure, then I suggest going back over *Power over Anxiety*. There are several examples to inspire you.
- Do things you enjoy. By doing things daily that you enjoy will make you happy and build your hope. What do you enjoy

doing? We have discussed this in a previous chapter. You might need to go back over the chapter to remind you.

- Perseverance—know many times it won't work, but have hope that you can learn from each fall-back and go back again better, stronger. How will you keep persevering?

Write your strengths. Everyone has strengths and talents. Write this down.

Be patient and persistent

I have built my hope by writing my achievements down and by reviewing what I have done. I have seen progress, something tangible to hold on to. I have a will to succeed, to have a better life for my family, and seeing my progress excites me for the future. My only problem now is that I want the future here, right now!

Why have hope?

For you to go forward, to keep going during the bad times, you need to have hope to know the pain will go. You can get better. But hope is something that can't be given. It can be grown slowly and from such a small glimmer of light. It's something you have to believe. It's faith that things can change and be better. They will!

Not to have hope, to feel hopelessness, is one of the saddest parts of anxiety. Because you need spirit and hope to improve your anxiety.

Repeat to yourself now. Several times. I have hope. I will save myself. I am going to get better!

I don't want to hear the words *'I am beyond help. I can't be saved'*. Because that's your anxiety talking not you.

Having hope pushes you beyond your limits. It gets you to believe everything will work out okay.

Better things are coming. Have hope!

What challenges will you face?

I encourage you to feel the hope you described at the start of this chapter. Let it wash over you. Take five minutes now to feel it. Then when you need this feeling. Use it again.

Don't forget!

- **Hope is a skill. It can be learned and developed.**
- **How do you want hope to feel like?**
- **Without hope you won't break anxiety. You can grow it from the tiniest seed. Don't tell me you are beyond help. YOU can be saved. And do you know who will save you? YOU WILL!**
- **Having hope will push you beyond your limits.**

Years on from the worse time of my life...

I take my dog for a walk in the woods. I breathe in. I take in the world as it is. I slow myself and watch the world go by. The sun sets in a glorious mixing of colour and light. I watch my dog run around smelling everything. This is his freedom. He loves this place.

I reflect on what has happened to my life in the last four years when I couldn't see a way out.

When all I could feel is pain. Life didn't matter. When I felt powerless, shame and rage. Rage at myself and the world.

I see the man I am and what I will become. I feel a pocket of pride come up. Like I made it to the other side. Like my pain meant something better.

I won my war. I did it. I clawed, struggled, cried, fell and fell again. So much pain. So much of my life with my head buried in the sh*t. But I kept getting back up. I beat my anxiety! I defeated it. Repeatedly!

I like the person I am. I have become someone I would have been proud of.

I look at the world completely differently now. Like it's there for the taking. Like there is nothing to fear. Like my anxiety has been a massive help to my life.

My war is over. My worst moments are over. I feel a release. A sense of power. Nothing can stop me in where I want to go.

I let my dog run off further than he should and I smile to myself. I look at what I have done over the last few years. Author of FIVE books, bestseller, helped thousands of people. Every day, I get messages from people needing hope.

If I knew what was on the other side. I would push even harder and earlier!

I want to show you where your life can be taken. My pain can guide you to a better place. Where I am now. Free from my own personal hell. And I did it. Little old me! You can do too!

Joy, Laughter & Anxiety

What do you want from this chapter?

Joy and laugher are other key components to put happiness back into
your life.

I have merged these two chapters into one from the original book.
Essentially, it is the same theme.

It seems an obvious one, yet it is probably the most difficult as you
really don't want to be laughing when you are in the throes of a very
scary, real panic attack. But laughter reduces the stress hormones that
come with anxiety. The effects are immediate and reduce anxiety
further. A great side effect of laughter and joy: higher energy levels and
happiness. I have read several articles on this subject. The claim is you
don't need medication or a long time to change.

When do you have time to take a laughter break, even for five minutes?

How do you want to feel when you laugh?

What does joy feel like to you?

When you laugh, observe the physical sensations of laughter. Write down here.

How do you feel afterwards?

How important is it to you to feel happy?

What skills will you use to let go and just feel the moment?

What are your favourite shows you love watching that make you laugh?

JOY in the Laughter

I always find that laughter with good friends the best. I feel pockets of joy. I like to have banter that is sometimes a little crude so I rarely get to chat with people that have a similar view. But when we do, it's awesome. Getting closer and feeling a sense of belonging. Sometimes we can be in hysterics laughing. Feel loads better afterwards.

Don't forget!

- Laughter really is the best medicine.
- Schedule time, Just five minutes a day, to let go and just laugh.
- Feel the joy in the laughter. Laughing is so much more than laughing. It can bring joy and happiness.

Music That Touches My Soul

I can get lost in music. Allowing the music to wash over me. This break out chapter is a simple one.

Listening to music is a great way of changing your mood and aids in you feeling happy. IF you listen to the right music.

Write down here how you feel when you listen to music.

What music makes you feel happy and pumps you up?

Make sure you take out ten minutes to your day to sing at the top of lungs your favourite songs. This will reduce your anxiety, fill with energy and release stress.

Write when you can do that each day. I do it in my car.

What are your favourite songs?
Write them down.

To My Old Self

Old me—I can't go on. There has to be more to life. I can't control myself. I can't control my emotions. I feel trapped, unable to escape the pain and torment. Leave me, leave me alone!

New me—Your life will get so much better. But you will suffer a little more. Hang in there. Life gets exciting!

Old me—*Ignores him. Too closed to his own pain and in total disbelief. Left to his own thoughts.*

New me—Hang in there. You will go beyond your fears. You will go years without a panic attack! Meeting some amazing people that will become good friends. You will help thousands. Yes! Thousands of people with their anxiety. Life is still a struggle, but what a huge change. Massive. Excited?

Old me—Really?

New me — Yes, really. And it all starts with hope!

If you could speak to yourself in the past, what would you say to them? Imagine it's you standing there a few years ago. What are you wearing? What is your body language?

What words would you say to yourself? Would you be supportive? Encouraging?

SOPHROSYNE

A healthy state of mind, Characterised by self-control, moderation, and a deep awareness of one's true self, and resulting in true happiness.

INSOUCIANT

Free from concern, worry, or anxiety; nonchalant.
—Dictionary.com

The Abyss — My Darkness

I have spent a lifetime of pain stuck in the abyss, with no light to guide me.

I have clawed up to the rim, fingernail by fingernail. Every second has felt like an eternity, living a life of hell. Not knowing what I was facing.

I have suffered; I have endured; I have felt lost and broken. Not deserving of love or happiness. All too often willing to sabotage what little good I have got.

I have felt it a curse, a humiliation of never feeling good enough.

The abyss, my darkness was my enemy, it anchored me, unable to escape. I was desperate, crushed and alone . . .

I haven't escaped the abyss; it stays by my side now, always telling me I am useless and not good enough. I observe these as only my thoughts.

My darkness reminds me that life is amazing, that you have seen the worse from life, from people. But you can also see the good.

It reminds me how important every moment is. It has shown me pain; now I see joy. See the appreciation of my world and my loved ones. To show my vulnerability and pain to help others.

I have never felt joy as intensely as I do now. My darkness drives me on, giving me the courage to face my fears. I am no longer desperate for my darkness to leave, but to be with me as I head towards the light.

My darkness reminds me how far I have come, and how much further I need to travel. I need my darkness by my side to be my better me.

The Humber Bridge

Showing how much I have improved—another milestone achieved!

I was taking a journey to Hull as part of my training. Off in the distance, I saw a huge bridge. The sun caught the giant columns, making them appear white. I looked out over the river. As I got closer I thought, *wow, that's captivating!*

Then the sudden realisation hit me: *Oh, my god I will have to drive over that!* A wave of blind panic and terror hit me. I could feel the start of an attack. The knots building in my stomach, the light feeling in my chest and head. I used my 7/11 technique and said to myself let's feel all my emotions and thoughts. Keeping myself anchored on my breath, I allowed them all to come at me...'*Just as you get on the bridge there could be a terrorist attack and blow up the bridge! You will die! Those struts could come off, and the bridge could collapse! That's you, dead!. What happens if you don't drive well and accidentally drive into the sea? It looks too tight for cars! What a way to die. Drowning in the river!*' I went to note them, but I realised I was smiling! My panic, my worry had dissipated. I was smiling at my own thoughts!

I got to the bridge and drove over it. I scanned over at the river below and took the whole view in; the huge river below almost looked like a sea, the countryside surrounding it. The families were walking together on the bridge and smiling. I took in the whole moment. Doing my 7/11, taking in all the beauty. It was a beautiful moment.

Once I had parked up a short distance later. I reflected on what had just happened. Even six months ago I would have had a panic attack. I would have driven over it, but I would have been scared witless. Now a massive milestone had been reached. Another important moment in my battle over anxiety. I had retaken control. I am pushing my anxiety back. I was so proud of myself! I made sure I celebrated this moment. I bought myself a chocolate bar. That's how I roll!

I have learned of late that the feelings of fear don't mean anything. My emotions cannot predict the future. If I feel fear, it's just an emotion. One to be tackled.

I felt elated. *Yes!* I thought. I can't believe it. I smiled at my thoughts.

That feeling of joy for the landscape and view. That elation for not having an anxiety attack—feeling less of a prisoner, made me feel on Cloud 9 for the rest of the day. I felt more self-confident. Building my hope more that I am going to be anxiety free soon.

A Reminder of the Man I Was

I had a night with little sleep. The following day was tough. My negative mind talk was back. Battering me all day. *'You are a failure. You are a fraud. Why are you doing this? You aren't good enough. Why are you even trying? Just give up.* I used my breathing to keep me calm. I listened to all the negative talk. My anxiety I could feel close to my chest. Threatening to break out.

I was so grateful for this day because it gave me an insight in to how I used to feel! It taught me how much I struggled, how far I have come and a newfound respect for the old me. My journal explained my feelings, but to feel them again was powerful.

I have the utmost respect for you that deal with anxiety. My arrogance expects more of myself. Not having the same expectations for others than I do myself.

I now have ways to cope with my anxiety. In the not too distant past, I didn't. I kept fighting on. I got punched around all day. Feeling low, feeling insecure, bereft of hope and any self-confidence.

This day gave me another teaching. To learn to forgive. To forgive the person I was. To not be so hard on him. To feel he wasn't good enough. To be proud of him he kept fighting on. Like I do with every single one of you.

The next day I felt happy all day. I felt relief. I had carried this baggage for a long time. To let it go took a weight away.

I wasn't that bad a man. I battled anxiety. And I got through it. Just like you will. Learn to forgive yourself.

How Do You Feel Right Now?

On a scale of one to ten? One feeling awful to ten feeling on top of the world! Rate how you feel on the following topics.

Find somewhere to record this. Keep it with you. These five points are the key to you feeling better. Focusing on them will help you. Seeing your score improve if you have followed this workbook. To where you were when you started this journey. Your progress!

Calm

Panic

Worry

Happiness

Confidence

Beliefs

This is a little different. Rather than doing a scale of 1 to 10. I want you to put whether you feel it's true or false next to the statement.

- I feel like a victim. Everything is my fault!
- What is wrong with me?
- I don't deserve the best life possible.
- I can't handle failure.
- I can handle rejection.
- I can't take criticism.

- If I work at it, I can have what I want.
- I am good enough.
- Life is too hard.
- Anxiety is too hard. I can't break it!
- Everyone hates me!

End Credits — On to Living the Life You Will Love and Become a Better You

---

'I breathe, deep breaths, slowly exhaling. I look out at the world around me and feel excited. My life is changing! I am breaking free. I feel in control of my life and nothing will stop me!'
— Christopher Moss

Congratulations! You have completed Hope over Anxiety Workbook!

It has been a great joy writing this to help and guide you.

After going through all the chapters you should feel empowered and ready to take on your anxiety. To take your life to new limits!

I am excited for you.

It all starts in drawing a line. Not falling back, going forward despite your anxiety pushing you back as hard as it can.

This battle to break through. Will take time, patience and love.

It all starts with a small glimmer of HOPE.

It starts with NO MORE! I stand here, and I won't go backwards. I will do this. I will break free. One foot forward each day!

You will find days that are tough; don't give up. Because those days will grow less and less. Each barrier you break, and each wall you break down, we get you closer to your end goal. To get to a life you never thought possible. Imagine a life where you can be anxiety free?

You have gone through all the steps. You have learned what your triggers are.

What laughter, joy and hope is.

I have not just set you up now. I want to set you up for an excellent future.

What you need to do now is practice. Tweak your structure to your day if you need to. Test, practice, test and practice.

What's the next step for you?

If you want me to help 1-to-1, then message me at mosschristopher799@gmail.com.

It's about pushing your own barriers have goals to hit and to go forward without falling back.

I hope you are now inspired and excited! Feeling a level of hope you have never felt.

You're armed with some excellent tools, skills and knowledge ready to take on anxiety. On your terms. Not accepting the old you, not accepting your anxiety's old tricks.

Ready to be the person you have always dreamed of!

I hope that you feel considerably calmer, and you have dropped in how much worry you have.

I am not here to give you tough or complicated steps to get out. I hope you understood what was needed and it has helped you.

Your new journey is just beginning.

Choose HOPE!

Want the first 6 chapters of my book Hope over Anxiety FREE?

Cool! Then email mosschristopher@gmail.com and say:

'Give me 6 free chapters please!'

The Best Reading/Anxiety Apps

The best apps:

Headspace – Guided and unguided meditations, track your progress and choose what you want to improve on. You can decide on everyday mediations, single, or projects.

Calm – Has guided meditations, calming nature pictures and sounds and has a meditation timer. There are some excellent very short meditations. Especially if you need one in an emergency. I would look out for the stories read by a host of well-known stars.

Did You Enjoy Hope over Anxiety Workbook?

If you enjoyed this book. I would greatly appreciate it if you could leave me a review.

I know your time is precious, but it will help me improve this book and my future adventures. It will only take a few minutes to do a sentence or two.

Your feedback will be warmly received.

Thank you,
Christopher Moss

My books!

I am very proud of my books. I have 5 out at the moment. If you would like to know more or would like more help on anxiety, then choose what book you would like to know more about.

Hope over Anxiety - Guides you on your journey from anxiety. You can pick and choose what chapter to read. An excellent companion to this book.

Freedom over Anxiety - Four simple steps to break free of anxiety.

Power over Anxiety - Cool hacks to the mind and body to break anxiety and feel the best you have ever felt!

Fearless Confidence - My shortest book. Simple and effective tools to be the most confident you have ever felt!

Keeping in Touch

I hope my story helped you, what I do on a day-to-day basis and the stories of others.

If you want further help and advice. You are more than welcome to visit:

Facebook – @CPMossauthor

Facebook group – Hope over Anxiety: Break your anxiety!

Email – mosschristopher799@gmail.com

I would love to hear from you about how this book has helped you.

Coach Call

Would you like further help and guidance? Do you wish to have one to one help from me? I give free first time 30 minute consultations.

Email to contact me. And you can choose a time to suit you. mosschristopher799@gmail.com

Crisis Centres

AnxietyUK — www.anxietyuk.org
The Sanctuary — www.selfhelpservices.org.uk
Rethink Mental Illness — www.rethink.org
No Panic — www.nopanic.org.uk

Facebook Groups

These are all the groups I am a member of. There are much more.

Those you can call on when you need help. They are all closed groups so only those that are in the group can see your posts allowing you to open up and share experiences.

Use the Facebook search engine and put these in:
Anxiety and Depression Support
Anxiety and Depression Support Group
Let's Talk Anxiety Group
Depression and Anxiety Safe Haven Support Group
Me, Myself and Anxiety

Acknowledgments

I am delighted with all those that have reached out to me over the last year, wanting to make the change for the better.

To my accountability partner Otakara Klettke.

To Jennifer Perez an amazing and inspiring woman that have made such a massive difference to so many people.

To my long-suffering wife who has put up with a lot of me with my head in the laptop writing over the last year.

To my VA Deanna Baxter. Been an amazing support. Thank you so much.

AND!

To you for your continued support. I write these books for you. To see that have helped others and that I get continued support from you is what keeps me going. YOU all rock!

Bibliography

What is anxiety?

Moodjuice.scot.nhs.uk
Anxietyuk.org.uk including studies on anxiety
Nomorepanic.co.uk

Self-confidence

The Mind Tools Content Team. "Building Self Confidence."
Mindtools.com
https://www.mindtools.com/selfconf.html

"Self-Esteem."
Mind.org.uk
https://www.mind.org.uk/information-support/types-of-mental-health-problems/self-esteem/#.XHoKC4hKjIU

Brené Brown – The Gifts of Imperfection

Gratefulness Diary

Henry, Alan. "Why You Should Keep a Journal (And How to Start Yours)." Lifehacker.com https://lifehacker.com/why-you-should-keep-a-journal-and-how-to-start-yours-1547057185

Obituary

Ismail, Karim H. *Keep Any Promise.* iUniverse, 2008.

Anxiety and Creativity

Brown, Brené. The Gifts of Imperfection. Hazelden Publishing, 2010.

Collard, Patrizia. The Mindfulness Bible: The Complete Guide to Living in the Moment. Walking Stick Press, 2015.

"Physical Exercise & Anxiety." Anxietyuk.org https://www.anxietyuk.org.uk/get-help/anxiety-information/physical-exercise-anxiety/

Mooney. Lisa. "How to Build Self-confidence and Eliminate Anxiety." Livestrong.com https://www.livestrong.com/article/173488-how-to-build-self-confidence-and-eliminate-anxiety

Laughter, Joy and Anxiety

Robinson, Lawrence; Melinda Smith, M.A.; and Jeanne Segal, Ph.D. "Laughter is the Best Medicine." Helpguide.org https://www.helpguide.org/articles/mental-health/laughter-is-the-best-medicine.htm

Bijou, Jude. "7 Ways To Create More Joy In Your Life." Mindbodygreen.com https://www.mindbodygreen.com/0-10143/7-ways-to-create-more-joy-in-your-life.html

Researching Crisis Centres and Best Apps

Blessing manifesting.com

High Performance Habits Brendon Burchard's book has inspired me throughout this book.

Burchard, Brendon. High Performance Habits. Hay House Inc., 2017

The Untethered Soul Michael A. Singer. Another amazing book and has inspired me throughout this book.

Singer, Michael A., The Untethered Soul: The Journey Beyond Yourself. New Harbinger Publications/Noetic Books, 2007.

Printed in Great Britain
by Amazon